Acknowledgements

The author would like to thank Erika Evans and Dahira Khalid for their help and support during the writing and production of this publication.

Mark Evans has been a teacher for over 25 years. He has taught in Australia, Japan, Malaysia and the UK. He graduated in languages from University College London and has a PGCE, CELTA, DELTA, Diploma in ESOL, as well as an MA in English Language Teaching. He currently lives in the UK where he teaches at a college and a university.

This edition published in London, England in 2020

ISBN: 9798649587877

Text copyright @2020, Mark Evans

No part of this book may be reproduced in any form, or by any means, without prior permission in writing from the author.

MeEducation

Please feel free to contact the author at - **meeducation@yahoo.com**

Please visit the website at **https://meeducation.net**

Also by the same author:

- Easy English
- SpeakEasy
- English Conversation Practice
- Idioms in English
- English for Work
- Pre Entry English
- Entry 2 Reading and Writing
- Entry 3 Reading and Writing
- Level 1 Reading and Writing
- Level 2 Reading and Writing
- Pre Entry Grammar (NEW!)
- Entry 1 Grammar
- Entry 2 Grammar
- Entry 3 Grammar
- Level 1 Grammar
- Level 2 Grammar (NEW!)
- Speaking Grammar
- English Vocabulary Builder

 ESOL King

Progression Routes for ESOL

Here are the progression routes for ESOL:

- Entry Level 1
- Entry Level 2
- Entry Level 3
- Level 1
- Level 2
- Level 3 (proposed)

The ESOL exams consist of three components:

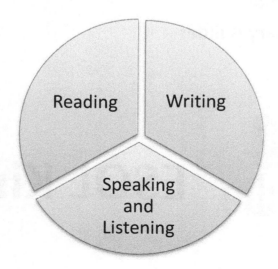

Contents

Recognising Letters of the Alphabet 1	7
Recognising Letters of the Alphabet 2	8
Capital to Small Letters 1	9
Capital to Small Letters 2	11
Symbols and Signs	13
Different Types of Text	15
Reading Notes	19
Reading a Receipt	21
Countries and Nationalities	22
Writing Capital Letters: Countries and Nationalities	23
Vowel and Consonants	24
Capital Letters	25
Capital Letters and Full Stops	26
Punctuation Mistakes 1	27
Punctuation Mistakes 2	28
Proofreading 1	29
Proofreading 2	30
Spellcheck 1	31
Write about Yourself	32
Literacy Check 1	33
Recognising Whole Words 1	34
Recognising Whole Words 2	35
Spellcheck 2	36
Personal Data	37
Filling in a Form: Registering for a GP	39
Filling in a Form: School Survey	40
Job Application Form	41

Work – Filling out an Application Form	43
Opening a Bank Account – Filling out an Application	44
Reading a Letter1	45
English Class – Filling out an Application Form	48
Reading a Letter2	49
Literacy Check 2	52
Spellcheck 3	54
Literacy Check 3: My Friend	55
Spellcheck 4	57
Reading and Writing an Email 1	58
Reading: The Coronavirus	60
Spellcheck 5	62
Reading and Writing an Email 2	63
Spellcheck 6	65
Reading and Writing an Email 3	66
Literacy Check 4	68
Reading and Writing an Email 4	69
Reading and Writing an Email 5	71
Articles	73
Reading Common Signs 1	74
Reading Common Signs 2	75
Recognising Familiar Symbols 1	76
Recognising Familiar Symbols 2	77
Speaking: Useful Phrases	78
Speaking: Taking Part in a Discussion	80
Maths: Maths Terms	82
Maths: Entry Level 1	84
Maths: Entry Level 2	87
Maths: Entry Level 3	91
Answer Key	97

Recognising Letters of the Alphabet 1

1) Here are capital letters. Circle the letters that are NOT capital letters:

A	b	C	D	e	F	g
h	I	j	K	L	M	N
O	P	q	R	S	T	U
V	w	x	y	Z		

2) Here are the small letters. Circle the letters that are NOT small.

A	b	c	d	e	F	g
h	l	J	k	l	M	n
o	p	q	r	s	T	u
v	w	x	y	z		

Now write the alphabet using capital letters:

Now write the alphabet using small letters:

Recognising Letters of the Alphabet 2

Here are the capital and small letters of the alphabet:

A a B b C c D d E e F f G g H h I i J j K k L l M m N n O o P p Q q R r S s T t U u V v W w X x Y y Z z

Write in the missing letters:

A a B b C c D _ E e F f G _ H h I i _ j K _ L _ M m _ n O o _ p Q q R r _ s T _ U _ _ v W _ X x _ y Z z

Now write the capital and small letters of the alphabet. The first one has been done for you:

A a
....
....
....
....
....
....
....

Capital and Small Letters 1

Here are words with capital letters. Match the words in small letters:

PEN	book
BOOK	teacher
SCHOOL	pen
TEACHER	college
FRIDAY	june
JUNE	school
COLLEGE	man
DOOR	friday
MAN	car
WOMAN	door
BANK	woman
CAR	bank
HELLO	hello
NAME	name
ADDRESS	phone
PHONE	address

(PEN is matched to pen with an arrow.)

Here are words with small letters. Match the words in capital letters:

book	DRINK
drink	FOOD
food	BOOK
eat	DRINK
drink	PEN
fish	PLAY
pen	EAT
door	FISH
play	MAN
man	DOOR
name	DATE
date	BANK
phone	NAME
address	HELLO
hello	ADDRESS
bank	PHONE

Capital and Small Letters 2

Here are words with small letters. Write the words in capital letters:

name	
address	
postcode	
age	
birth	
date	
phone	
number	
day	
week	
month	
school	
college	
work	
teacher	
student	
book	

Here are words with capital letters. Write the words in small letters:

NAME	
ADDRESS	
POSTCODE	
AGE	
BIRTH	
DATE	
PHONE	
NUMBER	
DAY	
WEEK	
MONTH	
SCHOOL	
COLLEGE	
WORK	
TEACHER	
STUDENT	
BOOK	

Symbols and Signs

Match the symbols and signs with the words:

$	And
£	Full stop
.	Morning
,	Happy face
am	Pound
pm	Afternoon/evening
&	Dollar
☹	Comma
☺	Plus/add
+	Bigger than/more than
-	Minus/subtract
X	Sad face
÷	Smaller than/less than
=	Equals
>	Times/multiplied by
<	Question mark
?	At
@	Divided by

Draw the signs and symbols next to the words:

And	
Full stop	
Morning	
Happy face	
Pound	
Afternoon	
Dollar	
Comma	
Plus/add	
Greater than	
Minus/subtract	
Sad face	
Less than	
Equals	
Times/multiplied by	
Question mark	
At	
Divided by	

Different Types of Texts

Identify these types of texts from their format.

Label: a leaflet, an email, a letter, a menu, a note, a receipt, a newspaper, a greetings card, a text message

1) _____

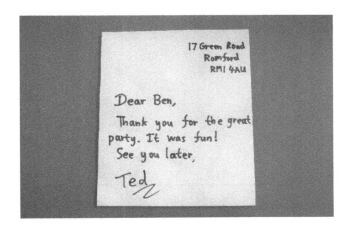

2) _____

3) _____

4) _____

5) _____

6) _____

7) _____

8) _____

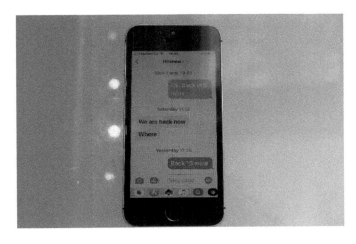

9) _____

Text Match

Where/when can you find these types of texts? Draw a line and match them:

A leaflet	On a computer
An email	In your letterbox
A letter	On your phone
A menu	On your birthday/at Christmas
A note	In a council office/school
A greetings card	In a shop
A text message	In a restaurant
A receipt	In a newsagent
A newspaper	At home, on the fridge

(A leaflet is matched with "In a council office/school" by an arrow.)

Reading Notes

1) The dentist appointment is on Friday   *Tick one box*

a   True

b   False

2) These are

a   emails

b   notes

c   letters

d   leaflets

3) They are going to meet Tom

a   in a shop

b   in a coffee shop

c   in a park

d   at the dentist

4) Underline two days of the week.

5) They are meeting Tom at 9 o'clock.   *Tick one box*

Yes ☐

No ☐

6) Which of these words matches the word APPOINTMENT? *Circle one*

   a   apointment

   b   appointmint

   c   appointment

   d   appointiment

7) What do they need to buy?

_____

8) Who are they going to meet?

_____

Reading a Receipt

Look at Bill's receipt and answer the questions below:

1) What is the name of the shop?

_____

2) Where is the shop?

_____

3) How many bananas did Bill buy?

_____

4) How much is each banana?

_____

5) Which item is reduced?

_____

6) How much is the total?

_____

7) How much change did Bill get?

_____

8) Underline all the fruit in the text.

Countries and Nationalities

Match the countries with their nationalities:

Great Britain	Spanish
Spain	French
China	Syrian
Poland	British
Japan	Romanian
France	Polish
Syria	Iraqi
Romania	Chinese
Iran	Japanese
Iraq	Iranian

(Great Britain → British)

Writing Capital Letters: Countries and Nationalities

Write the capital letters in these sentences:

1) I come from Britain. I am british.

....

2) I come from Poland. i am polish.

....

3) i come from syria. I am Syrian.

....

4) I come from china. I am Chinese.

....

5) i come from spain. i am Spanish.

....

6) I come from Romania. i am romanian.

....

Write about you. Where do you come from? What is your nationality?

....

Vowels and Consonants

Write the vowels in the box:

Write the consonants in the box:

Answer the questions:

1) What is your name?

_____

2) How many vowels are there in your name?

_____

3) How many consonants are there in your name?

_____

4) What country are you from?

_____

5) How many vowels are there in your country's name?

_____

6) How many consonants are there in your country's name?

_____

Capital Letters

Write capital letters in the correct place:

1) my friend's name is Tom.

....

2) he lives in oxford in england.

....

3) he lives at 55 park street and his postcode is ox3 5be.

....

4) his birthday is in january.

....

5) he speaks english, french and a little arabic.

....

6) he comes from durban in south africa.

....

7) tom is married to a lady called linda.

....

8) they have two children called jim and jill.

....

9) his hobby is watching tv.

....

10) tom's favourite programme is called mastermind.

....

Capital Letters and Full Stops

Copy the text below and put in capital letters and full stops:

myfriendsnameisellasheistwentyfiveyearsoldellalivesinlondonsheisachefinarestaurantsheismarriedtobillybillyisateacherheworksataschoolinlondontheyhavetwochildrentheirnamesaredannyandmariadannyissevenyearsoldandmariaissixyearsoldellalikesshoppingandcookingshedoesntlikeplayingfootballshehastwosistersandonebrotherilikemyfriendella

....

....

....

....

....

....

....

....

....

....

....

....

....

Punctuation Mistakes 1

Correct the mistakes with punctuation and capital letters in the sentences below:

1) next spring i am Going to france

....

2) its going TO be a nice Day on saturday

....

3) are we going to See john in the uk

....

4) i studied english With my friend tom yesterday

....

5) the tower of london is Next to the riVer thames

....

6) i went to hyde parK in london

....

7) I love spanish fooD

....

8) why didnt YOU visit peter in Manchester last week

....

9) i didnt watch tv last night

....

10) im not happy because i cant find my dvd

....

Punctuation Mistakes 2

Correct the mistakes with punctuation and capital letters in the sentences below:

1) i like eaTing french fOOd

....

2) my friend ken Learns japanese every day

....

3) does sarah like Her house in the united states

....

4) what time is the Next train to oxford

....

5) my friends cat is caLLed tiger

....

6) i went to holland park IN london

....

7) i can cook spanIsh fOOd but not chineSe food

....

8) ben and maria run in the Park every morning

....

9) adam Likes cooKing indian food

....

10) i listen to Music on my cd player

....

Proofreading 1

Find the grammar and spelling mistakes in the sentences below then correct them:

1) Their is many cups in the room.

....

2) I am go to the park evry day.

....

3) My frind is like play footbal.

....

4) Lucinda is long hair.

....

5) My friend her name is Cindy.

....

6) Yasmin go to shopping every days.

....

7) Zara is no like go to the beach.

....

8) I can to drive a car.

....

9) There are one bus at the bus stop.

....

10) You can buy some fruit for me in the supermarket?

....

Proofreading 2

Find the grammar and spelling mistakes in the sentences below then correct them:

1) My friend went to shopping and bought many cake.

....

2) I meet my frind Yuko in the park

....

3) She is cook rise every day.

....

4) What you did last weekend?

....

5) My fiend can rides a bike

....

6) Terry and Peter lives in nice flat.

....

7) I am go usually to schol by bus.

....

8) Eric work in a supermarket with he friend Ted.

....

9) I going to meet my friend tonight.

....

10) Can you buy tow apple, thre banana and a pineapple

....

Spellcheck 1

Circle the correct spelling:

1	naam	name	nam	nayme
2	com	come	cam	comme
3	englan	england	England	Engeland
4	liv	live	livv	leve
5	yer	yar	year	yir
6	auld	old	olde	ould
7	techar	teecher	ticher	teacher
8	marrid	mareed	marride	married
9	childran	childsren	children	childrin
10	futball	feetball	football	footbill

When you have finished, check your answers in the text in the box on the next page and write the correct spelling below:

1)	2)
3)	4)
5)	6)
7)	8)
9)	10)

Now write the words in alphabetical order:

Write about Yourself

Read the story and answer the questions:

My name is David. I come from England. I live in Richmond. I am 33 years old. I am a teacher. I am married. I have two children. I like football.

1) How many sentences are there?

2) Underline the full stops. How many full stops are there?

3) Why do we use full stops?

4) Circle all the capital letters. How many capital letters are there?

5) When do we use capital letters?

Now write about yourself:

Literacy Check 1

Correct the mistakes in the text below. Correct the:

- *Capital letters*
- *Full stops*
- *Spelling*
- *Grammar*

> my nam is peter hill i am a techar i works in a schol in london i live on oxford road in camden i am 47 yers olde my favourit foode is pizza and mye favourit drink is coffe i am marrid and I have tow children i like playing tennis and walking in the parc

Copy the correct version of the text above into the box below:

Recognising Whole Words 1

Separate the whole words in the text below and write them out:

Everydayigetupat7amthenigodownstairsandeatbreakfastieattoastandaneggidrinkacupofteawithmilknextihaveashowerandgetdressedthenileavethehouseanditakeabustocollegeatcollegeistudyenglishat9:30amihavelunchat12:30ieatasandwichigohomeat4pm

Write here:

....

....

....

....

....

....

....

Now write about what you do every day in the box:

Recognising Whole Words 2

Separate the whole words in the text below and write them out:

Lastweekendimetmyfriendandwewenttotheparkwewenttoacafeintheparkandd rankcoffeetogetheritwasfunafterwewentshoppingandboughtsomeclothesafter shoppingitookthebushomeathomeicookeddinnerformyfamilyweatefishandricei twasdeliciousthenwewatchedtvfortwohourswewenttobedat10pm

Write here:

....

....

....

....

....

....

....

Now write about your last weekend in the box and use a dictionary to check your spelling:

Spellcheck 2

Circle the correct spelling:

1	naam	name	nam	nayme
2	title	titel	tietel	teetel
3	addres	address	adres	adresse
4	werk	worke	work	werke
5	jobe	jobbe	job	jobby
6	school	skool	schol	skole
7	maniger	manager	maneger	miniger
8	boss	bos	bosse	bose
9	silery	salery	salary	selery
10	exsperience	experiance	expiriance	experience

When you have finished, find the words in the job application on the next page and check your answers. Then write the correct spelling below:

1)	2)
3)	4)
5)	6)
7)	8)
9)	10)

Now write the words in alphabetical order:

Personal Data

Match the information below:

First name — Smith
Surname — Australia
Address — 65 Bill Street, London
Post code → Wade
Phone number — NW1 8SQ
Age — 2/6/68
Date of birth — 07745 444 345
Country of birth — Running
Marital status — English and French
Languages — 52
Hobby — Married

*Now fill in the form about **you**:*

First name …………………………………….

Surname   …………………………………….

Address   …………………………………….

Postcode   …………………………………….

Phone no. …………………………………….

Age   …………………………………….

Date of Birth …………………………………

Country of birth ……………………………

Marital Status (*circle*)   single   married   divorced

Language …………………………………….

Hobby   …………………………………….

Match the questions and answers below:

What's your first name?	Smith
What's your surname?	The UK
What's your address?	55 Park Street, London
What's your post code?	John
What's your phone number?	W12 8QT
How old are you?	5/5/70
What's your date of birth?	07745 388 123
Where are you from?	Playing football
Are you married?	English and Arabic
What languages do you speak?	50
What is your hobby?	Yes, I am

*Cover the questions and look at the answers. Ask **your partner** the questions and fill out the form below:*

```
First name ………………………………….
Surname   ………………………………….
Address   ………………………………….
Postcode  ………………………………….
Phone no. ………………………………….
Age       ………………………………….
Date of Birth ……………………………...
Country ……………………………………..
Marital Status (circle)    single    married    divorced
Language ………………………………….
Hobby     ………………………………….
```

Job Application Form

Read the information about Steve below:

My name is Steve Bacon. I come from London, England. I speak English and a little French. I live at 55, Park End Road, Camden, London, NW1 6SP. I was born 6th May 1969. I went to Camden High School. I worked in Tesco supermarket for 5 years. I was a supervisor. I am friendly and reliable.

*Now fill in the **missing** details:*

- Title: Mr
- Surname: Bacon
- First name: ……………………………….
- Male or Female: ……………………..
- Date of Birth:………………………….
- Nationality: British
- Address:
- House number:……………………...
- Street: Park End Road
- Town/City: ………………………………
- Postcode:………………………………..
- Work experience:……………………………………………………………………………
  ……………………………………………………………………………………………………
- Education:
  ……………………………………………………………………………………………………
- Languages: English and ……………………………………………………………………

Now write information about yourself:

Now fill in the details:

- Title: ……………………
- Surname: …………………………………
- First name: …………………………………
- Male or Female: ……………………
- Date of Birth:……………………………
- Nationality: …………………………….
- Address:
- House number:………………………
- Street: ………………………………….
- Town/City: …………………………….
- Postcode:…………………………………..
- Work experience:………………………………………………………………………………………
  ……
- Education:
  ……
- Languages: …………………………………….

Filling in a Form: Registering for a GP

Fill in the registration form:

Richmond Surgery
First Name:
Surname:
Address:
Postcode:
Telephone Number:
Nationality:
Date of Birth:
Signature:

Filling in a Form – School Survey

Fill in the school survey:

Title (**Circle one**)	Mr Mrs Miss Ms
First name	
Surname	
Address	
City	
Telephone number	
Email address	
Date of Birth	
Signature	
Date	
Do you like your school? (**Circle one**) no a little so so yes very much	

Work – Filling Out an Application Form

Title: _____ First Name (s): _____   Last Name: _____

Date of Birth: _____

Gender: (Circle)   Male   Female

Address:

_____

_____

_____

Postcode: _____

NI number: _____

Previous Positions:

```
┌──────────────────────────────────────────────────────────────┐
│                                                              │
│                                                              │
└──────────────────────────────────────────────────────────────┘
```

Education:

```
┌──────────────────────────────────────────────────────────────┐
│                                                              │
│                                                              │
└──────────────────────────────────────────────────────────────┘
```

References:

```
┌──────────────────────────────────────────────────────────────┐
│                                                              │
│                                                              │
└──────────────────────────────────────────────────────────────┘
```

Contact Details:

Mobile Phone: _____   Email Address: _____

Opening a Bank Account – Filling Out an Application Form

Fill out this form:

Title: ___ First Name (s): _____ Last Name: _____

Date of Birth: _____

Gender: (Circle)   Male   Female

Address:

_____

_____

_____

Postcode: _____

Time at Current Address: _____

NI number: _____

Marital Status: _____

Occupation: _____

Nationality: _____

Country of Birth: _____

Contact Details:

Home Phone: _____

Work Phone: _____

Mobile Phone: _____

Email Address: _____

Reading a Letter 1

Read Paula's letter to her new teacher and answer the questions about it:

> 12 Green Street
> London
> W12 8QT
> 23/7/20
>
> Dear Mr Brown
> Hi! I am your new student. My name is Paula. I come from Spain. I have one brother and one sister. I am learning English because I want to get a job in London. I want to be a chef in a restaurant. In my free time I like playing football. My favourite food is fish and rice.
>
> Your student
>
> Paula

1) What kind of text is it? *Circle the correct answer.*

Email   Letter   Form

2) Who wrote the letter?
_____

3) What is Paula's address?
_____

4) When did Paula write the letter?
_____

5) Who did Paula write the letter to?
_____

6) Where does she come from?
_____

7) How many brothers does she have?
_____

8) How many sisters does she have?
_____

9) Why is she learning English?
_____

10) What job does she want to do?
_____

11) What does she like to do in her free time?
_____

12) What is her favourite food?
_____

Write a letter introducing yourself to your teacher. Write:

- your name
- where you are from
- about your family
- where you live
- why you are studying English
- what job you want to do in the future
- what you like doing in your free time

English Class – Filling out an Application Form

You want to apply for a course at the local college. Fill out this form with your details:

First Name:
Surname:
Male　　　　Female　　(circle)
Address:
Postcode:
Date of Birth:
Date:　　　　　　　　　　　　Signature:

Reading a Letter 2

Flat 6
8, Calm Street
London
NW2 4SX
17/4/20

Dear Class

Hello! How are you? My name is Sarah Smith and I am 26 years old. I am from London, England. I live on Calm Street. I am a student.

Please write to me and tell me all about yourselves.

Kind regards

Sarah

A: *Read the text and answer these questions:*

1) What kind of text is this? (circle)

Email   Letter   Form

2) How do you know the answer?

_____

3) Who wrote it and how do you know?

_____

4) Where is she from?

_____

5) How old is she?

_____

6) What is her postcode?

_____

7) What is her job?

_____

B: *The information below is wrong. Correct it:*

1) Her name is John Gray.

2) She is 32.

3) She is Swedish.

4) Her address is 30, Calm Road.

5) She is a teacher.

C: Answer the questions:

1) How many capital letters are there in the letter?

_____

2) When do we use capital letters?

_____

3) How many full stops are there?

_____

4) How many sentences are there in the letter?

_____

5) What does Sarah want?

_____

Now write a letter introducing yourself below:

Literacy Check 2

Correct the mistakes in the text below. Correct the:

- *Capital letters*
- *Full stops*
- *Spelling*
- *Grammar*

Flat 6
8, calm street
london
nw2 4sx
17/4/20

dear Class

Hello? How are you my nam is sarah smith and I am 26 year old I am from london, england i live on calm stret i am student

Please writ to me and tel me all about yourselves

kind regards

sarah

Check your answers on the previous page. Next, copy the correct version of the text above into the box below:

Spellcheck 3

Circle the correct spelling:

1	mothar	mother	mather	mothere
2	father	fathor	farther	fathar
3	brothar	brother	brovar	brothere
4	sister	seester	sistar	sustar
5	frind	frand	freind	friend
6	Yer	yeer	year	yeare
7	weekende	weekend	weekand	weakend
8	football	footballe	feetball	fitball
9	park	perk	parke	parkk
10	Saterday	Saturdey	Saturdiy	Saturday

When you have finished, check your answers in a dictionary and write the correct spelling below:

1)	2)
3)	4)
5)	6)
7)	8)
9)	10)

Now write the words in alphabetical order:

Literacy Check 3: My Friend

Correct the mistakes:

my Best frend's name is ben. His 40 yers old. he live in greenwich in london. he work in a banke in London. he have one brother. His name is steve.

we meet every week. We talk about footballs and work.

His hobby is footbal. he play every saturday in the Park with his frinds. i lik me best frind very much!

Copy the correct version and write it below. Next use a dictionary to check:

Questions

1) What is a vowel?

2) What is a consonant?

3) Circle all the vowels in the last sentence in the text on the last page.

4) How many vowels are there in the last sentence?

5) Underline the consonants in the last sentence.

6) How many consonants are there in the last sentence?

Now write about your best friend:

Spellcheck 4

Circle the correct spelling:

1	picnic	picnik	picnice	peeknic
2	tommorow	tomorow	tomoro	tomorrow
3	wehter	weather	wither	weathar
4	suny	sonny	sony	sunny
5	come	com	kome	comme
6	starte	startt	start	stirt
7	plis	pleese	please	plese
8	bring	brinng	bringe	brinng
9	foood	food	foode	fud
10	drinke	drik	drink	drenk

When you have finished, check your answers in the email on the next page and write the correct spelling below:

1)	2)
3)	4)
5)	6)
7)	8)
9)	10)

Now write the words in alphabetical order:

Reading and Writing an Email 1

Read this email and answer the questions:

From: Peter
Hi I am having a picnic in King's Park tomorrow. Tomorrow the weather is sunny. Bill and Fred can come. Can you come? We start at 11am. Please bring food and drink. What food can you bring? Bye Peter

1) Who wrote the email?

_____

2) What day is the picnic?

_____

3) Where is the picnic?

_____

4) What time is the picnic?

_____

5) Who can come?

_____

6) What does Peter want you to bring?

_____

You can go to the picnic. Write a reply. What food and drink can you bring? Write four or more sentences:

Send	

Reading: The Coronavirus

Identify the complete sentences by putting in capital letters and full stops:

1) coronavirus is a virus which started in china you can catch it when people sneeze or if you touch infected places the symptoms can be a dry cough or a fever to prevent the virus always wash your hands when you come home and before you eat food

Now write the correct version below:

2) *Answer the questions:*

(a) What does symptom mean? Circle the correct answer:

"sign" or "place"

(b) What does prevent mean? Circle the correct answer:

"stop" or "start"

3) *Answer the questions:*

(a) Where did coronavirus start?

(b) How can you catch it?

(c) What are the symptoms?

(d) How can you prevent it?

4) *Answer the questions:*

(a) How many vowels are there in the word "prevent"? Circle them.

(b) How many consonants are there in the word "symptoms"? Circle them.

5) *Identify these types of texts:*

To prevent coronavirus, wash your hands before you eat and when you get home. Contact the NHS for further information.	If you get symptoms of coronavirus, do not visit your GP or go to hospital. Call 111 and the NHS will advise you what to do.

What type of texts are these? *Circle the correct answer:*

Email

Leaflet

Letter

Greetings card

Menu

Newspaper

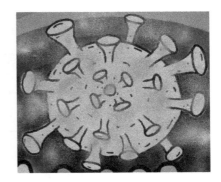

Spellcheck 5

Circle the correct spelling:

1	stayshon	station	statien	staton
2	butiful	beautifull	beautiful	beautifal
3	tow	two	twoo	twoo
4	bedroom	badroom	bedrom	bedroome
5	kitchon	kitchan	kichen	kitchen
6	windoow	window	wendow	windew
7	bathroom	bathrom	bafroom	bathroome
8	showar	showir	shawar	shower
9	toilat	toilit	toilet	toilete
10	plise	pleas	please	plese

When you have finished, check your answers in the email on the next page and write the correct spelling below:

1)	2)
3)	4)
5)	6)
7)	8)
9)	10)

Now write the words in alphabetical order:

Reading and Writing an Email 2

Read this email and answer the questions:

From: Linda
Hi I have a new flat! It is near the station. It is beautiful. There are two bedrooms. One bedroom is big and one is small. There is a large living room and there is a nice kitchen. The kitchen has a big window. Also, there is a bathroom with a shower and a toilet. I love my new flat! Please write to me and tell me about your flat. Bye Linda

1) Who wrote the email?

_____

2) Where is the flat?

_____

3) How many bedrooms are there?

_____

4) Which room has a big window?

_____

5) How many rooms are there?

_____

6) Does she like her new flat?

_____

Write a reply below. Write about the place where you live. Write four or more sentences:

Send	

Spellcheck 6

Circle the correct spelling:

1	arear	area	ereya	areer
2	ofice	offise	office	offece
3	suparmarket	sopermarket	supermarkat	supermarket
4	tow	two	twoo	towo
5	three	thre	threee	toree
6	chuche	chursh	church	churc
7	coffe	coffee	kofi	koffee
8	resturunt	restarant	restrunt	restaurant
9	delicias	delicious	dalicious	delichous
10	ples	pleese	pleas	please

When you have finished, check your answers in the email on the next page and write the correct spelling below:

1)	2)
3)	4)
5)	6)
7)	8)
9)	10)

Now write the words in alphabetical order:

Reading and Writing an Email 3

Read this email and answer the questions:

From:	Bob
Subject	My Area

Hi!
I am living in a new area now called South Park. It is a nice area. There is a post office, a big supermarket, a park and a church. There are two pubs and three coffee shops. There is also an Italian restaurant with delicious food. Please tell me about your area.
See you soon,
Bob

1) Who wrote the email?

_____

2) Where does he live?

_____

3) Is it a nice area?

_____

4) How many coffee shops are there?

_____

5) How is the food in the Italian restaurant?

_____

6) What does Bob want you to do?

_____

Write a reply. Tell Bob about your area. Write four or more sentences:

Send	

Literacy Check 4: My Town

Correct the mistakes:

i liv in a nice town my town iss very cleane. Their is a bigg park with a beautifal lake. Their are many shops. You can buying fod and cloths.

Their are sefen restunts. There are italian, chinese and french restrunts i like italain best. There is thre pubs and tow churches.

There is a stashon with treins to london. There are mony buss stops. i lik me town very much!

Copy the correct version below:

Reading and Writing an Email 4

Read this email and answer the questions:

From:	Mark
Subject	Class is starting!

Hi
How are you? The college is now open. We are going to start class next Monday. We start at 9:30. Bring your ID and your books. Can you come?
Bye
Mark

1) Who wrote the email?

_____

2) What day is the college?

_____

3) Where is the class?

_____

4) What does Mark want you to bring?

_____

5) How many sentences are there?

_____

6) How many words are there?

_____

You can't go to the class. Write a reply. Why can't you go to the class? Write four or more sentences:

Send	

Reading and Writing an Email 5

Read this email and answer the questions:

From:	Carina
Subject	Lunch with a friend

Hi
How are you? I am at my friend's house. I am eating lunch. I like pasta. What do you like to eat? What are you doing now?
See you soon.
Carina

1) Who wrote the email?

_____

2) Where is she?

_____

3) What is she doing now?

_____

4) What does she like?

_____

5) How many sentences are there?

_____

6) How many words are there?

_____

Write a reply to Carina. Answer her questions. Write four or more sentences:

Send	
....	
....	
....	
....	
....	
....	
....	
....	
....	
....	

Articles

Write "a" "an" or "-" (for no article) in front of these nouns:

1) bed
2) egg
3) chair
4) song
5) glass
6) letter
7) cat
8) orange
9) book
10) class
11) old man
12) website
13) extremely nice man
14) good day
15) funny joke
16) unusual lady
17) expensive car
18) hard exercise
19) interesting film
20) wonderful life

Recognising Common Signs 1

Put these signs in pairs:

open	pull
push	closed
entrance	gentle men
ladies	exit

(arrow drawn from "open" to "closed")

Recognising Common Signs 2

| PULL | No Entry | OUT OF ORDER |

| Entrance | Ladies | Lift |

| Queue here | No Smoking | Gents |

Write the signs next to the meaning:

1) You can go in here:

2) You can't go in here:

3) You can't smoke here:

4) You can go up and down floors here:

5) Men can go to the toilet here:

6) Women can go to the toilet here:

7) Stand and wait here:

8) This does not work:

9) Pull this door to open:

Recognising Familiar Symbols 1

Work in pairs. What do you think the signs below mean?

 (a)  (b)  (c)

 (d)  (e)  (f)

 (g) (h)

Match the symbols with the instructions:

School: ……………………………..

No Entry: ……………………………..

Parking: ……………………………

No Cycling: ……………………………..

Cycling ok: ……………………………

Emergency Exit: ………………………

Bus Stop: ……………………………

20 mph speed limit: ……………….

Recognising Familiar Symbols 2

Draw labels and match the words below with the symbols above:

First Aid   Fire Exit   No Entry

Way Out   No Smoking   Not Drinking Water

         Danger   Wet Floor

Speaking: Useful Phrases

Asking for Someone's Opinion

What do you think of…?

What's your opinion on…?

Giving your Opinion

I think…

In my opinion…

Agreeing and Disagreeing

I think so too.

I agree with you.

I don't agree with you.

Adding a Point

And another thing,

Also…

Likes and dislikes

I like…

I don't like…

Interrupting

Sorry, but...

Sorry to interrupt, but...

Pausing and Hesitating

Let me think about that for a minute.

That's a good question.

Hmm...

Well...

Asking for Clarification

What do you mean?

Could you explain in more detail, please?

Does it mean...?

What does _____ mean?

Giving Advice

You should...

You shouldn't...

Speaking: Taking Part in a Discussion

You are going to take part in a discussion with one other person.

You need to communicate clearly with another person.

You need to ask questions to check understanding.

You need to recognise non-verbal information given by another person.

You need to take turns.

You need to have a discussion.

Task 1

Talk about food you like and don't like with another student.

You must ask questions. You could talk about:

- food you like and don't like.
- things you can cook.
- how often you cook.
- who cooks in your house.
- food in your country.

Task 2

Talk about your neighbourhood with another student.

You must ask questions. You could talk about:

- where you live.
- if you live in a house or flat.
- places in your neighbourhood.
- your neighbours.
- good and bad things about your area.

Task 3

Talk about living in the UK with another student.

You must ask questions. You could talk about:

- where you live.
- why you came to the UK.
- your favourite place in the UK.
- your dreams for your life in the UK.
- a job you want in the UK.

Task 4

Talk about your free time with another student.

You must ask questions. You could talk about:

- what you do in your free time.
- where you spend your free time.
- who you meet in your free time.
- how often you have free time.
- a hobby you want to do.

Task 5

Talk about shopping with another student.

You must ask questions. You could talk about:

- if you like/don't like shopping.
- where you go shopping.
- shops in your area.
- where a good place to shop is.
- who shops in your house.

Maths: Maths Terms

Match the words with the shapes:

Square   Triangle   Rectangle   Cylinder   Circle   Cube   Cuboid   Sphere

Match the words to the symbols:

Plus   Subtract   Add   More than   Less than   Equals
Greater than   Multiply   Smaller than   The same as   Divided by
Times   Minus   Take away

+   _____, _____

-   _____, _____, _____

×   _____, _____

÷   _____,

>   _____, _____

<   _____, _____

=   _____, _____

Self-check

Draw a square...   Draw a circle...

Draw a triangle...   Draw a rectangle...

Draw a cube...   Draw a cuboid...

Draw a sphere...   Draw a cylinder...

Write the sign for plus... _____

Write the sign for minus... _____

Write the sign for divide... _____

Write the sign for multiply... _____

Write the sign for greater than... _____

Write the sign for less than... _____

Questions

1) What is a total?

2) What is a fraction?

3) What is a right angle?

4) How many sides does a cube have?

5) How many edges does a triangle have?

Maths: Entry Level 1

Counting

Tick the pens.

How many pens are there?

How many pens and pencils are there in total?

Are there more pens or pencils?

Time

Draw a clock in the box showing the time of 3pm.

Comparing

Tick the smallest food:

What is the name of the food on the left?

What is the name of the food on the right?

Shapes

In the box draw a circle, a triangle, a square, a rectangle, a cube and a cuboid:

Calculations

Ken goes for a bike ride once a week. How many times does he go in a month?

Bill buys a mask for £10 and a filter for £2. How much does he pay in total?

He pays with a £20 note. How much change does he get?

Tick the change he gets.

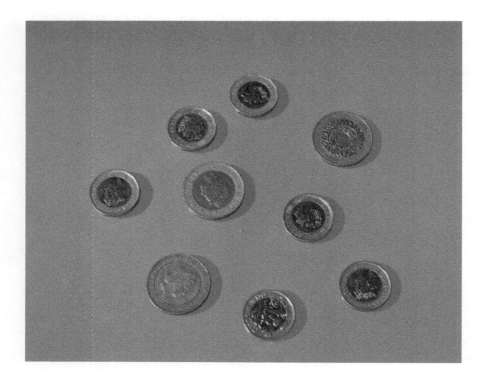

Maths: Entry Level 2

Steve has a shop and he ordered mobile phones and they will be sent to his shop on Saturday 30th May 2020.

Circle the date the phones will be sent to his shop.

30/6/20   5/30/20   30/5/20   20/5/30

The mobile phones will come in boxes.

Box 1 = 25 phones
Box 2 = 30 phones
Box 3 = 15 phones

Which box has the most phones?

How many phones are there in total?

If he doesn't buy box 3, how many phones will he have? *Show your workings.*

The boxes are rectangular shape. How many edges does one face of the box have?

Steve's shop is open from 9:30 to 4:30. How long is the shop open?

Draw a clock with 9:30 on it:

Steve sends some phones to his customers in other countries:

Columbia = 8

Japan = 12

Hong Kong = 18

How many phones go to Columbia?

Which country gets the most phones?

When he sends them to Hong Kong, he chooses the widest box. Which box is the widest? *Circle the widest box.*

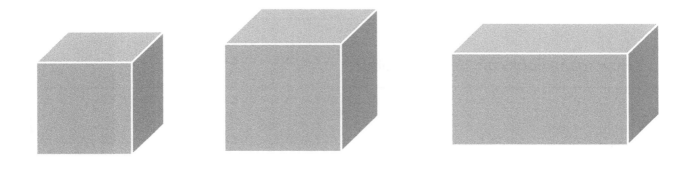

Mark writes his own books and sells them on the Internet.

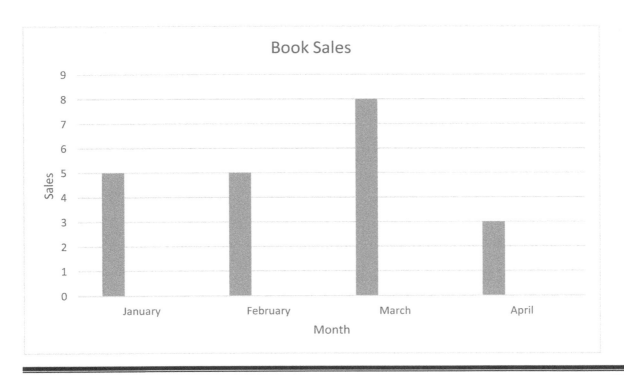

Put the information from the chart into this table:

How many more books did he sell in March than in April?

How many books did he sell in total?

4 out of the 8 books sold in March were bought by one person. What fraction is this?

Last week Mark sent his book in boxes of 8.

Book	Book	Book	Book
Book	Book	Book	Book

Shade in ¼ of the boxes above.

What fraction of the boxes above is not shaded?

Maths: Entry 3

Sue goes to work by bike. She leaves at 8:50. It takes her 15 minutes. Draw a clock below with the time she arrives:

Linda walks to work. She needs to start at 9am. It takes her 45 minutes to get to work. What is the **latest** time she can leave her house?

Linda sells computers. She sells these computers in one month:

Ringo = 15

Ichigo = 34

Meron = 23

Suica = 13

Linda wanted to sell over 100 computers last month. Did she do this? **Show your working:**

$\frac{2}{3}$ of the Ringo computers were black. What fraction were **not** black?

Which **two** fractions are equivalent to $\frac{2}{3}$? Tick 2 answers:

A ( ) $\frac{2}{6}$

B ( ) $\frac{4}{6}$

C ( ) $\frac{8}{12}$

D ( ) $\frac{3}{2}$

12 boxes were delivered last year. Each box contains 11 computers. How many computers were ordered **in total**? **Show your working:**

11 kg

Measure the longest edge of the box above. Write your answer in the box below:

How many right angles are there on one face on the box?

Linda weighs the box on an electronic scale. She has to pay a fee if it weighs more than 10kg. Does she have to pay a fee?

Linda's company also sells batteries. There are 12 batteries in one box. A customer ordered 15 boxes. How many batteries is this in total?

Each box weighs 3.3kg. What is the total weight of the customer's order?

Round the weight up to the nearest 10.

Draw the lines of symmetry on the box below.

Linda sends a box from the company in Richmond to a customer in Colchester. Which direction is Colchester from Richmond?

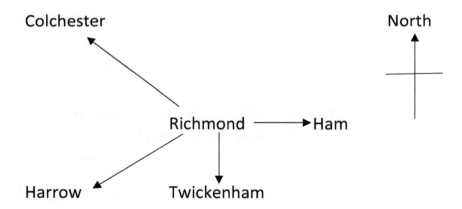

She sends one box to Colchester, 5 boxes to Twickenham, 8 boxes to Ham and 15 boxes to Harrow. Complete the table below to show how many boxes she sent to each place.

Town	Number of boxes sent
Colchester	
Ham	
Harrow	
Twickenham	

A customer goes to the shop in Richmond and buys a Ringo computer. They pay £384 over 2 years in equal monthly payments. How much is this every month?

Another customer in the Richmond shop buys headphones for £19, a mouse for £15 and a mouse pad for £5. They pay with two twenty pound notes. How much change will they get?

The company decides to offer a free USB stick to every 15th customer. Fill in the chart below:

Customer number	15	30		
USB given	1	2	3	4

Computer Name	Weight
Ringo	2kg
Ichigo	2.5kg
Meron	3.4kg
Suica	4kg

The company makes a new computer which is 200g lighter than the lightest computer. How heavy is it? **Show your workings.**

Answer Key

Recognising Letters of the Alphabet 1

1) b, e, g, h, j, q, w, x, y

2) AFMT

ABCDEFGHIJKLMNOPQRSTUVWXYZ

abcdefghijklmnopqrstuvwxyz

Recognising Letters of the Alphabet 2

d, g, J, k, l, N, P, S, t, u V, w, Y

Different Types of Text

1) Greetings card 2) Letter 3) Menu 4) Newspaper 5) Leaflet 6) Email 7) Note 8) receipt 9) Text message

Email – on your computer, letter – in your letterbox, menu – in a restaurant, note – at home, greetings card – on your birthday, text – on your phone, receipt – in a shop, newspaper – in a newsagent

Reading Notes

1) True 2) b, notes 3) c, in a park 4) underline Friday and Tuesday 5) Yes 6) c, appointment 7) milk, eggs & coffee 8) Tom

Reading a Receipt

1) Tesco 2) Twickenham, London 3) 5 bananas 4) Strawberries 5) £11.05 6) £4 7) underline strawberries, banana

Vowels and Consonants

Vowels: a,e,i,o,u

Consonants: b,c,d,f,g,h,j,k,l,m,n,p,q,r,s,t,v,w,x,y,z

1-5 Various answers

Capital Letters

1) My friend's name is Tom. 2) He lives in Oxford in England. 3) He lives at 55 Park Street and his postcode is OX3 5BE. 4) His birthday is in January. 5) He speaks English, French and a little Arabic. 6) He comes from Durban in South Africa. 7) Tom is married to a lady called Linda.

8) They have two children called Jim and Jill. 9) His hobby is watching TV. 10) Tom's favourite programme is called Mastermind.

Capital Letters and Full stops

My friend's name is Ella. She is twenty five years old. Ella lives in London. She is a chef in a restaurant. She is married to Billy. Billy is a teacher at a school in London. They have two children. Their names are Danny and Maria. Danny is seven years old and Maria is six years old. Ella likes shopping and cooking. She doesn't like playing football. She has two sisters and one brother. I like my friend Ella.

Punctuation 1

1) Next spring I am going to France. 2) It's going to be a nice day on Saturday. 3) Are we going to see John in the UK? 4) I studied English with my friend Tom yesterday. 5) The Tower of London is next to the River Thames. 6) I went to Hyde Park in London. 7) I love Spanish food. 8) Why didn't you visit Peter in Manchester last week? 9) I didn't watch TV last night. 10) I'm not happy because I can't find my DVD.

Punctuation 2

1) I like eating French food. 2) My friend Ken learns Japanese every day. 3) Does Sarah like her house in the United States? 4) What time is the next train to Oxford? 5) My friend's cat is called Tiger. 6) I went to Holland Park in London. 7) I can cook Spanish food but not Chinese food. 8) Ben and Maria run in the park every morning. 9) Adam likes cooking Indian food. 10) I listen to music on my CD player.

Proofreading 1

1) There are many cups in the room. 2) I go to the park every day. 3) My friend likes playing football. 4) Lucinda has long hair. 5) My friend's name is Cindy. 6) Yasmin goes shopping every day. 7) Zara doesn't like going to the beach. 8) I can drive a car. 9) There is one bus at the bus stop. 10) Can you buy some fruit for me in the supermarket?

Proofreading 2

1) My friend went shopping and bought many cakes. 2) I met my friend Yuko in the park. 3) She cooks rice every day. 4) What did you do last weekend? 5) My fiend can ride a bike. 6) Terry and Peter live in a nice flat. 7) I usually go to school by bus. 8) Eric works in a supermarket with his friend Ted. 9) I am going to meet my friend tonight. 10) Can you buy two apples, three bananas and a pineapple?

Spellcheck 1

1) name 2) come 3) England 4) live 5) year 6) old 7) teacher 8) married 9) children 10) football

Write about Yourself

1) 8 sentences. 2) 8 full stops. 3) To finish a sentence. 4) 11 capital letters. 5) At the beginning of the sentence and names of people and places.

Literacy Check 1

My name is Peter Hill. I am a teacher. I work in a school in London. I live on Oxford Road in Camden. I am 47 years old. My favourite food is pizza and my favourite drink is coffee. I am married and I have two children. I like playing tennis and walking in the park.

Recognising Whole Words 1

Every day I get up at 7am. Then I go downstairs and eat breakfast. I eat toast and an egg. I drink a cup of tea with milk. Next I have a shower and get dressed. Then I leave the house and I take a bus to college. At college I study English at 9:30am. I have lunch at 12:30. I eat a sandwich. I go home at 4pm.

Recognising Whole Words 2

Last weekend I met my friend and we went to the park. We went to a café in the park and drank a coffee together. It was fun. After we went shopping and bought some clothes. After shopping I took the bus home. At home I cooked dinner for my family. We ate fish and rice. It was delicious. Then we watched TV for two hours. We went to bed at 10pm.

Spellcheck 2

1) name 2) title 3) address 4) work 5) job 6) school 7) manager 8) boss 9) salary 10) experience

Personal Data

Surname – Smith, Address – 65 Bill Street, London, Post code – NW1 8SQ, Phone – 045444345, Age – 52, Date of birth – 2/6/68. Country of birth – Australia, Marital status – married, Languages – English & French, Hobby – running

What's your surname – Smith, What's your address? – 55 Park Street, London, What's your postcode? – W12 8QT, What's your phone number? – 07745388123, How old are you? – 50, What's your date of birth? – 5/5/70. Where are you from? – The UK, Are you married? – Yes, I am, What languages do you speak? – English and Arabic, What's your hobby? – Playing football

Job Application Form

Steve; Male; 6/5/69; 55; Camden, London; NW1 6SP; Worked in Tesco supermarket for 5 years; Camden High School; French

Reading a Letter 1

1) Letter. 2) Paula wrote the letter. 3) Her address is 12 Green Street, London, W12 8QT. 4) She wrote the letter 23/7/20 5) She wrote the letter to Mr Brown. 6) She comes from Spain. 7) She has one brother. 8) She has one sister. 9) She is learning English because she wants to get a job in London. 10) She wants to be a chef. 11) She likes playing football. 12) Her favourite food is fish and rice.

Reading a Letter 2

A: 1) Letter 2) The address is at the top. 3) Sarah because her name is at the bottom of the letter. 4) She is from London, England. 5) She is 26 years old. 6) NW2 4SX 7) She is a student.

B: Her name is Sarah Smith. 2) She is 26 years old. 3) She is English/British. 4) Her address is 8 Calm Street. 5) She is a student.

C: 1) 26 2) At the start of a sentence and the names of people and places. 3) 5 full stops. 4) 6 sentences. 5) She wants to know about other people.

Literacy Check 2

>   Flat 6
>   8, Calm Street
>   London
>   NW2 4SX
>   17/4/20
>
> Dear class
> Hello! How are you? My name is Sarah Smith and I am 26 years old. I am from London, England. I live on Calm Street. I am a student.
>
> Please write to me and tell me all about yourselves.
>
> Kind regards
>
> Sarah

Spellcheck 3

1) mother 2) father 3) brother 4) sister 5) friend 6) year 7) weekend 8) football 9) park 10) Saturday.

Literacy Check 3: My Friend

My best friend's name is Ben. He's 40 years old. He lives in Greenwich in London. He works in a bank in London. He has one brother. His name is Steve. We meet every week. We talk about football and work. His hobby is football. He plays every Saturday in the park with his friends. I like my best friend very much!

1) Vowels: a,e,i,o,u 2) Consonants: b,c,d,f,g,h,j,k,l,m,n,p,q,r,s,t,v,w,x,y,z 3) **I like** my be**st fri**e**nd** v**e**ry m**u**ch! 4) 8 vowels. 5) I like my best friend very much! 6) 17 consonants.

Spellcheck 4

1) picnic 2) tomorrow 3) weather 4) sunny 5) come 6) start 7) please 8) bring 9) food 10) drink

Reading and Writing an Email 1

1) Peter wrote the email. 2) It's tomorrow 3) It's in Kings Park. 4) It's at 11am 5) Food and drink.

Reading: The Coronavirus

1) Coronavirus is a virus which started in China. You can catch it when people sneeze or if you touch infected places. The symptoms can be a dry cough or a fever. To prevent the virus always wash your hands when you come home and before you eat food.

2) a) sign b) stop

3) a) It started in China. b) You can catch it when people sneeze or if you touch infected places. c) The symptoms can be a dry cough or a fever. d) To prevent the virus always wash your hands when you come home and before you eat food.

4) a) 2 vowels. b) 7 consonants.

5) Leaflet

Spellcheck 5

1) station 2) beautiful 3) two 4) bedroom 5) kitchen 6) window 7) bathroom 8) shower 9) toilet 10) please

Reading and Writing an Email 2

1) Linda wrote the email. 2) It is near the station. 3) There are two bedrooms. 4) The kitchen has a big window 5) There are five rooms. 6) Yes, she does.

Spellcheck 6

1) area 2) office 3) supermarket 4) two 5) three 6) church 7) coffee 8) restaurant 9) delicious 10) please

Reading and Writing an Email 3

1) Bob wrote the email. 2) He lives in South Park. 3) Yes, it is. 4) There are three coffee shops 5) It is delicious. 6) He wants us to tell about our area.

Literacy Check 4

I live in a nice town. My town is very clean. There is a big park with a beautiful lake. There are many shops. You can buy food and clothes. There are seven restaurants. There are Italian, Chinese and French restaurants. I like Italian best. There are three pubs and two churches. There is a station with trains to London. There are many bus stops. I like my town very much!

Reading and Writing an Email 4

1) Mark wrote the email. 2) It's on Monday. 3) It's at college. 4) He wants you to bring ID and books. 5) 6 sentences. 6) 31 words.

Model answer:

> Hi Mark
> How are you? Sorry, I can't go to college. I have an appointment with the doctor. I am sick.
> See you soon.
> Eugenio

Reading and Writing an Email 5

1) Carina wrote the email. 2) She is at her friend's house. 3) She is eating lunch. 4) She likes pasta. 5) 7 sentences. 6) 32 words.

Model answer:

> Hi Carina
> How are you? I am fine. I like to eat fish. Fish is good. I am studying now. I am at college.
> See you soon.
> Eugenio

Articles

1) a 2) an 3) a 4) a 5) a 6) a 7) a 8) an 9) a 10) a 11) an 12) a 13) an 14) a 15) a 16) an 17) an 18) a 19) an 20) a

Reading Common Signs 1

push > pull; entrance > exit; ladies > gentlemen

Reading Common Signs 2

1) fntrance 2) No entry 3) No smoking 4) Lift 5) Gents 6) Ladies 7) Queue here 8) Out of Order 9) Pull

Recognising Familiar Symbols 1

School – c; No Entry – h; Parking – g; No Cycling – e; Cycling OK – d; Emergency Exit – f; Bus Stop – a; 20 mph speed limit - b

Recognising Familiar Symbols 2

From left to right: Wet floor, No Entry, First Aid, Not Drinking Water, No Smoking, Fire Exit, Way Out, Danger.